Through These Eyes

Through These Eyes

CURT BAKER

Through These Eyes
Copyright © 2021 by Curt Baker. All rights reserved.

No part of this publication may be reproduced, stored in a retrieval system or transmitted in any way by any means, electronic, mechanical, photocopy, recording or otherwise without the prior permission of the author except as provided by USA copyright law.

The opinions expressed by the author are not necessarily those of URLink Print and Media.

1603 Capitol Ave., Suite 310 Cheyenne, Wyoming USA 82001
1-888-980-6523 | admin@urlinkpublishing.com

URLink Print and Media is committed to excellence in the publishing industry.

Book design copyright © 2021 by URLink Print and Media. All rights reserved.

Published in the United States of America

Library of Congress Control Number: 9781647535568
ISBN 978-1-64753-556-8 (Paperback)
ISBN 978-1-64753-557-5 (Digital)

02.11.20

Contents

Sunsets 7
All Over Again 8
Adjust Your Sail 9
A Strange Journey 10
A night at home 11
A Good Ole Fishing Hat 12
You Are My World 13
Written in the stars 14
Winter is Drawing Nigh 15
Where Would You Go 16
Where we all Dwell 17
When I was boy 18
We Danced in the Rain 19
Waist Deep in Splendor 20
This View 21
Things I will never forget 22
The Quiet Realm of Solitude 23
The Reason I Go 24
The Poem of the Ocean 25
The Heat 26
The Fall Story 27
The Colors of Life 28
The Beauty of the Night 29
The Beauty of Nature 30
Tell Me Something Beautiful 31
Sunshine touched my soul 32
Soothe My Soul 33

Title	Page
Play on our Drummer	34
Paradise	35
Paradise with you	36
Our Little Gang	37
Oh How I do Miss	38
Nature's Calling	39
My Favorite place	40
My Destination	41
My Amazing Life	42
Love Abounds	43
Just Be Free	44
Just A Few Things I love	45
It's Winters Turn	46
It Will All Go Away	47
It was always you	48
Incredible Treasure	49
In This House Dwells a Dog	50
In Our Dreams	51
In my Arms	52
I'll be Alright	53
I'll always Love You	54
I Sometimes Wish	55
I Remember When	56
I Love the Summer	57
I Love the Night	58
I just need to get away	59
How Beautiful	60
Food for Your Mind	61
Enjoy the Wine	62
Engrave My Soul	63
Coffee Cup	64
At the Park	65
At Night	66
Asleep in our Bed	67

Sunsets

I feel so loved, when I'm with you,
I feel there's nothing I can't do.
The way I feel when you hold me tight,
Lets me know, everything's alright.

On the beach with your hand in mine,
The stars above us twinkle & shine.
The Glistening moon set on the sea,
Lets me know, you're the one for me.

Glad I made you my beautiful Wife,
I want to share with you my life.
Together we'll be for eternity,
Just open your heart & you will see.

Only the heart knows when it's right,
When love is true it's a beautiful sight.
When we're together there's nothing wrong,
Love with you is a beautiful song.

Spend my days with your hand in mine,
When we're together I feel so fine.
There's just one thing that I must do,
I want to spend the rest of my Sunsets with you.

To my Beautiful Wife Lori
From the luckiest man in the World.

All Over Again

The moon was a sliver in the dark night,
Blue lit stars made a beautiful sight.
The stillness of the night was so serene,
It was as if I was in a dream.

The night time air was crisp with a chill,
Surrounded by darkness it was very still.
A bullfrog bellowed out his lullaby,
A distant owl hooted in the night sky.

The lamplight gave off an eerie glow,
With millers & moths skittering to & fro.
The fireflies flashed in the night time air,
Then moved on, without worry or care.

At night mother earth is very much alive,
Waiting patiently as the sun arrives.
Then a brand new day starts to begin,
And she does it all over again.

Adjust Your Sail

When this world pours out to you it's wrath,
It's time to navigate your own path.
When life charges like a runaway horse,
We adjust our sails & alter our course.

Life will knock you down a time or two,
Getting back up is really up to you.
It's easy to fail in this troublesome fight
When you just can't see an end in sight.

Know that the storms, just don't last.
So have no fear & stand fast!
Have courage to face the ill winds,
Stand tall no matter what it sends.

Fight & you will make it through,
This is something you must do.
I know at times many will fail,
Just remember to adjust your sail.

A Strange Journey

As I slept one night so serene,
It seems I had a fisherman's dream.
Somehow I traveled back in time,
To fly fish our land in it's prime.

There were no highways or cities too,
I fished our land while it was new.
The air was pure and the water clean,
Breathtakingly beautiful and so pristine.

All I could do was stand in awe,
As I took in the beauty of what I saw.
Somehow I couldn't believe my eyes,
That's when I suddenly realized.

It all changed before me as I stood,
And reverted back to where it should.
I awoke and was saddened by then,
When I think back on what might have been.

A night at home

The fire gave off its eerie glow,
We sipped our wine very slow.
The weather outside was a wintry storm,
But beside the fire we stayed quite warm.

Silently the snow fell with nary a sound,
As if it had been painted to cover the ground.
We sat in silence if truth be told,
Enjoying the serenity as it began to unfold.

The glasses gave a ring as we raised a toast,
To the silence & beauty that we like the most.
Soothing to the soul with no sorry nor care,
Relished the quiet togetherness that we shared.

It was a wonderful night & so serene,
As if an artist had painted the scene.
Some Fridays it's nice to get out & roam,
But this was a wonderful night at home.

A Good Ole Fishing Hat

I know women will never understand,
The importance of a fishing hat to a man.
It is a valuable part of his fishing garb,
Just like a hook with or without a barb.

It may be a brand new one that catches his eye,
Or maybe his favorite, the old standby.
There is even his famous lucky one,
That will be on him to fish in the sun.

I know we have lost them several times over,
Gone back and found it lying in the clover.
The wind has blown them off into the river,
We recovered them wet and wore them with a shiver.

This phenomenon could never be explained,
I have tried and she only complained.
I guess only a fisherman knows that,
There's nothing like a good OLE fishing hat

You Are My World

In these maddening times of loves lost,
Love comes and goes regardless of cost.
We both have been down that beaten path,
Lived the uphill climb and the aftermath.

Somehow, someway we did survive,
We both found out that true love is alive.
I really don't know how it all came about,
Whether it was fate or coincidence or what route.

Somehow through it all we found us,
Although a few around us threw quite a fuss.
For a moment I thought you would flee,
That you would live your life without me.

Through a twist of fate, you made way to my heart,
Since then I knew we would never be apart.
As our hearts were strangely yet happily curled,
I want you to know that you are truly my world.

Written in the stars

I often wonder how this all came to be,
The love that we share just you & me.
I'm not certain when exactly It came,
Or how it happened & who's to blame.

My love for you has endless depths,
It grows daily, with every step.
You have filled my heart with so much,
Often it starts with just a touch.

I know for certain that you changed my life,
That's why I wanted to be Husband & Wife.
My love has depths that I never knew,
And it was all, because of you.

I knew our love is a special thing,
That everyday makes my heart sing.
It makes me happy this love of ours,
For I know it was written in the stars.

Winter is Drawing Nigh

Time itself passed by so quickly it seems,
Often times it's as if we're living in our dreams.
Here today & gone tomorrow,
Leaving us with great sorrow.

The greens of summer are a mere thought,
The warmth of the sun and the fun it brought.
It quickly faded into our past,
Although we hoped that it would last.

With summer's passing, October is upon us all,
This means that we are heading into the fall.
The splash of colors adorn our trees,
Picturesque with the changes to their leaves.

But now the leaves are almost fallen down,
The crisp fall air is no longer around.
The bone chilling air means fall has passed by,
That means winter is drawing nigh.

Where Would You Go

If you had a chance to go anywhere and fish
Where would you fulfill your wish?
Would you go out West for cutthroat Trout?
Or up North to Alaska where the Salmon are stout?

Maybe you would go to Canada to fish for Pike,
Perhaps to Wisconsin for Mushy if you like.
Down to Texas where the big Bass are,
Even Pennsylvania where the Brookies star.

Up in Minnesota where the Walleye rule,
Or to Colorado where the air is cool.
You may prefer to oceans deep,
Where the bigger fish are yours to keep.

It seems to me there are choices to make,
Of where to go and what gear to take.
There are so many places that I wouldn't know,
But where do you think you would go?

Where we all Dwell

I would like for you to do something for me today,
Please listen to what it is I have to say.
I'm hoping it will be all worth your while,
Maybe even make you smile.

I want you to be still & just breathe the air,
Take notice of the simple things so fair.
Just be at peace & let your mind mend,
Smell the rain & feel the wind.

Look to the sky so blue & bright,
The emerald trees just add to the sight.
Feel the warmth of the sun on your face,
Just notice everything around this beautiful place.

Maybe you will feel more at ease,
As the wind blows it's soft gentle breeze.
It's such a privilege to be alive & well,
To be happy on this earth that we all dwell.

When I was boy

I was contemplating just the other day,
Thinking about my life back in the day.
The things we used to find to play with,
Looking back it all seems as a myth.

I'll give you some examples & you will see,
Maybe you had them just like me.
I'll just name a couple maybe one or rwo.
But actually there were quite a few.

Two clothespins made a fine gun,
Played cops & robbers in the mid day sun.
We made us a fabulous sword,
That was made from an old board.

A jump rope we made from a clothesline,
That someone didn't need at the time.
A garbage can lid made a fine sled,
We slid down the ditch until time for bed.

We played for days with a cardboard box,
Now all they do is stay in & play x box.
Back in the day, the outside was our toy,
That's how I remember being a boy.

We Danced in the Rain

It was a perfect rainfall in June,
I remember that it was around noon.
No thunder & no lightning at all.
Just a soft continuous downward fall.

On our phone played some really good songs,
Ones that we quite often sing along.
You sat on the other side of the room,
Peering through the window out at the gloom.

All of a sudden & out of the blue,
Our song came on and I knew just what to do.
I took hold of your hand & led you outdoors,
And we danced as it continued to pour.

You softly whispered this is a first for me,
You'll love it I said, just wait & see.
The drops tapped on the window pane.
I held you close & we danced in the rain.

Waist Deep in Splendor

The gentle flowing river was so serene,
So I took time to look over the scene.
The fog had lifted from the waters top,
The dew from the trees made a continuous drop.

I stood in awe at this never-ending peace,
That my heart knew it would never cease.
I silently breathed and watched even more,
As the rapids below, sounded its roar.

In dawns early light the river came alive,
The trout leaped then continued its dive.
I watched a beaver swim to & fro,
To the edge for a drink came a buck & a doe.

The ducks & geese swam silently by,
Some took to flight high in the sky.
I waded in deeper as the minnows scattered,
A red squirrel watched then began to chatter.

I witnessed the river as it awoke from its sleep,
And I knew this memory I would forever keep.
Standing in the river I'll forever remember,
As I silently stood, waist deep in splendor.

This View

My morning coffee on my front lawn,
I watched as the sun cracked the dawn.
I witnessed as the Earth awoke from it's sleep,
A memory I knew I would forever keep.

The springtime air had a familiar smell,
It was a scent that I remembered so well.
The birds were the first ones to arrive,
They flew to & fro up in the sky.

Their chirping & song filled the air,
Filling my world with sounds so fair.
The cooing of the dove from a distant tree,
Was a lullaby that felt just for me.

I silently enjoyed this wonderful sight,
When everything around me was just right.
I hope you had the chance to see it too,
Perhaps I will share this view with you.

Things I will never forget

I remember growing up as a young lad,
Times were good & sometimes bad.
But through it all we made it through,
I remember fondly things we used to do.

There was always a ball game near & far,
Red rover & tag in the back yard.
Hide & go seek well after dark,
The 9:30 curfew beside the school park.

I recall all the games we used to play,
Poison & 7up, hopscotch & tag all day.
So many games I can't name them all,
But often they included some kind of ball.

A friend had told me these words to say,
Those times made us what we are today.
He was right about that & you can bet,
These are things I'll never forget.

The Quiet Realm of Solitude

Sometimes alone is the best place to be,
Where you can escape life & just be free.
Contemplate the many things that's on our plate,
How we can clear our thoughts & change our fate.

The silence can be a welcoming guest,
From the hustle & bustle of life at it's best.
When the World around us gets too loud,
It's an amazing way to avoid the crowd.

It's not a place for you to dwell,
But a refuge for your soul, to get well.
I often go there to free my mind,
To find peace & quiet of any kind.

So when life around you gets a bit too much,
And the world around you get's hard to touch.
When all you get from life is attitude,
Just visit the quiet realm of solitude.

The Reason I Go

The Wineries that we have found,
Are wonderful places to be around.
Where we enjoy a glass or two,
And meet with friends who like it too.

We venture out no matter what the seasons,
To each winery for different reasons.
Each one of them has their individual charms,
Whether they're city chic or garden farms.

Often they're decked out in some theme,
A Rockwell Christmas or Halloween.
It's the wonderful people that we've met,
Who give a hearty welcome, you can bet.

The people, wine & the unique decor,
Are the reasons we go back for more.
But it's the Wine I want you to know,
Is the real reason that I go.

The Poem of the Ocean

If you ever get to visit the ocean,
Sit and watch the waves commotion.
She has her own story to tell,
And she tells it very well.

If you can just for a moment,
Be still & listen for your enjoyment.
The methodical waves, have a verse & rhyme,
Listen with your heart and hear it every time.

Her words are beautiful if you dare,
She will free your mind of worry & care.
She speaks directly to your soul,
A calming reason is her goal.

The surf, the sand and the breeze,
Will transform & put your troubles at ease.
Close your eyes and feel her motion,
Then you'll capture the poem of the ocean.

The Heat

I'm very anxious to get outside in the sun,
Cookout & swim and have some fun.
It's been a long winter don't you agree?
Being couped up inside just isn't for me.

The cold chills of winter just get old,
If you venture outdoors you will get cold.
My skin is so dry & itches bad,
It's enough to make anyone mad.

I'm not usually one to complain,
But old man winter drives me insane.
You huddle up together in some shape or form,
Hoping that both of you will keep warm.

It won't be long then it will be spring,
The flowers will sprout & the birds will sing.
Yes, at last winter has finally been beat,
Then we can complain about the heat.

The Fall Story

Geez it's almost Labor day,
I'm quite surprised, I have to say.
Summer it seems has just flown by,
It's sad to me I thought with a sigh.

The leaves are slightly turning hues,
It seems as time has just flew.
Gone are the days spent in the pool,
Soon the kids, will be off to school.

The early mornings have a chill,
The Dew on the grass, the air still.
Fall is approaching, it's in the air.
As the cycle turns, without a care

I love the many things about the fall,
The splash of colors on the trees so tall.
I will miss the Summer & it's glory,
But the Fall is a different story.

The Colors of Life

I think of the colors that surround our days,
And how they make us feel in various ways.
Like the seasons they come & go,
Some linger with us while others no.

Sometimes we can't see what's been done,
Seems life is just to busy for everyone.
From winter through the year & into fall,
The colors change our lives after all.

The grays of winter & the whites of snow,
That gives way to spring & it's thawing flow.
Look at the beauty of the different hues,
The emerald greens & the summer blues.

The yellow colors of the mid day sun,
Surrounding us with warmth until it's done.
The black sky at night & stars way up high,
Blue & silver they shine in the sky.

Yellow, orange & browns paint our trees,
Then the fall scatters them with its chilly breeze.
The colors of the seasons help with our strife,
Yet no one seems to notice the colors of life.

The Beauty of the Night

I often like to stand alone after the evening gives way,
When the fowl has ceased their chatter at the end of the day.
The gentle calm & stillness has taken hold of our land,
The stars and moon have come out just to make their stand.

The fireflies have appeared as they start their nightly dance,
I stood transfixed & breathless as the
night they did enhance.
A wonderment of peace as I watched it all unfold,
Their lights flashed in the darkness as small flakes of gold.

The cool night time air is crisp & full of scent,
The fruit trees are joined by a slight hint of mint.
A breeze gave the motion as the trees gently swayed,
I pondered on leaving but I was happy that I stayed.

I gazed upon this serenity as time seemed to stand still,
And I smiled to the heavens knowing this was all his will.
I will never forget how I felt or the incredible sight,
As I silently stood before,,,, the beauty of the night.

The Beauty of Nature

Is our God an artist? I believe he may be,
All around us his beauty we can see.
We just need to view it all,
From the winter months into the fall.

A new fallen snow that blankets our land,
Always a beautiful sight for any man.
Many artists have captured this scene,
The cold crisp nights are so serene.

The Spring brings the earth back to life,
Ending the icy grip, of winter's strife.
The flowers in bloom & greeting the sun,
The budding trees begin their incredible run.

Summer shows us a different story,
The wildflowers & gardens are all in their glory.
The fireflies & butterflies flutter to & fro,
The hummingbirds & dragonflies come & go.

But the fall is indeed God's greatest prize,
The trees adorned with color as a new sunrise.
Splashes of gold, yellow, red & green,
Is as beautiful as anything I've ever seen.

The brightest skies with the clearest blues,
The oceans deep and their amazing hues.
The pearly whites of the majestic glaciers,
This, my friends, Is the beauty of nature.

Tell Me Something Beautiful

It seems at times life can beat you down,
Problems & hard times are always around.
Sometimes no matter what you do,
It appears it's not enough and it gets to you.

Wife came home & breathed a heavy sigh,
She also had tears forming in her eyes.
She rushed to my arms as I held her tight,
I knew that things were not quite right.

You wouldn't believe the day I've had,
She looked up at me & was very sad.
She laid her head down on my chest,
I'm so glad I'm home & you're the best.

As I held her close, time stood still,
She said, I need you to tell me if you will.
Life is so cold & I'm tied of this game,
Tell me something beautiful, so I whispered out her name.

Sunshine touched my soul

The morning sun's rays was soothing on my skin,
So I decided to just sit there & take it all in.
It felt so good after winter's firm icy grip,
It was nice to know the season began to flip.

I took the time to look around,
There was plenty of rebirth & growth found.
The daffodils rose up out of their slumber,
They too loved the suns wonder.

It appears that I was not alone feeling this way,
All of God's creatures enjoyed this day.
Their songs & chatter one could hear,
It's a soothing sound that I hold dear.

The warmth of the sun was a gift to behold,
Once it relieves you from the winter's cold.
I sighed a breath, as the clouds began to roll,
Never forgetting when the sunshine touched my soul.

Soothe My Soul

When I feel burdened under life's heavy woes,
You are always there, to keep me on my toes.
Whenever the stress is just too much for me,
You seem to know the ways, just to set me free.

When despair is knocking at my door,
You break it down until there is no more.
Every day you save me, but you don't really know.
It is because of you, that I continue to grow.

I can face my fears and even stand tall,
Because I know you'll be there if I ever fall.
Through life's raging storms & wind,
You have helped me, until their very end.

You are my gift in this place we call life,
I'm so thankful that you are my Wife.
Whenever this life starts to take its toll,
You are always there, just to soothe my soul.

Play on our Drummer

One chilly December morning,
You left us all here with little warning.
On that day our hearts did cry,
When you departed and said good bye.

The tears in our eyes & pain in our hearts,
That each one of us will never part.
The drummer we all loved was gone,
But in each one of us, his beat lives on.

We wished we had more time with you,
That one last song, we wanted to do.
It was not to be I'm sad to say,
But we knew you were with us on that day.

So play your drums let the cymbals ring,
Play your drums as the Angels sing.
For "the Gang" did not, say good bye,
Just "later" till we meet, in the sky.

The time and the seasons, they will pass,
Soon the snow will turn to grass.
Spring will lead us to our summer,
until then, play on our drummer.

Paradise

I watched from afar as she walked in the sand,
The breeze tossed her hair as if it were fanned.
She strolled slowly as the waves lapped her feet,
The water cooler her from the sun's summer heat.

She looked at peace as she walked with ease,
She had no purpose, just walked as she pleased.
Her soul was free that you could tell,
The sea cleanses your thoughts, very well.

Her silhouette was kissed by the setting sunlight,
I was happy I could witness this beautiful sight.
As she turned towards me & continued her pace,
A smile had caressed my lips & face,

She returned to me where I was set,
Kissed me & said this is as good as it can get.
We were in paradise, this much is true,
Of course paradise is who you have beside you.

Paradise with you

I wish to sail the seven seas,
Guided by the ocean breeze.
Feel the salty mist on my face,
As I sailed off to some exotic place.

The tranquility of a sandy isle,
Is sure to make anyone smile.
The palm trees swaying in the wind,
A troubled soul it would mend.

Surrounded by various tropical fruits,
Coconuts gathered by the palms roots.
The turquoise water & white Sandy beach,
Paradise is definitely within my reach.

A grass hut in a private lagoon,
Would indeed make my heart swoon.
But it wouldn't be a dream in the ocean blue,
If I didn't share my paradise with you.

Our Little Gang

There is a small group of friends,
That I will love to the very end.
The laughs & lives that we shared,
Is nothing that can ever be compared.

Looking back, it all seemed so short,
The times we spent on a basketball court.
The barn, the girls & the parties we had,
When we were all very young lads.

Some memories that I am quite fond,
Like camping out by Millers pond.
The music & memories that we made,
From our lives will never fade.

How cool we were with our "LOVE" T-shirts,
That we wore, going to church.
We were wildcats & wore them proud,
We liked to stand out in a crowd.

Here we are now many years from then.
Still together and we're all still friends.
Someday when the last song is sang,
We will all remember our little Gang.

Oh How I do Miss

The scent of the beach as the sun rises,
The beauty of the sea & all of her surprises.
The dolphins greeted me as I watched them play,
The gulls & pelicans flew by and made their way.

The lapping of the gulf was music to my ears,
Against the distant horizon stood a fishing pier.
The morning sun caresses my face as it gently rose,
It seemed to erase all of those worldly woes.

The seashells were scattered all along the shore,
The gentle breeze of summer added even more.
Nothing can compare to the peace & calm,
I watched it all unfold from the shade of a palm.

Sitting in my chair, watching the snowflakes fall,
Reminds me of being there & how I miss it all.
Reminiscing of the sunset as the sea it did kiss,
Just made me realized of oh how I do miss.

Nature's Calling

Mother nature fills our lives with such wonderful sounds,
The serenade of our fowl indeed has no bounds.
All we have to do is listen & quietly be still,
Here are some of my favorites, so join me if you will.

I miss the sound of a whip- poor-will in the Forrest air,
His distinct whistle is indeed quite rare.
The Bob White calls out his name for all to enjoy,
Its whistle has been copied by every girl & boy.

The honking of Canadian geese as they fly above,
Is a sound you've heard & I'm sure you truly love.
The quacking of a mallard as he sits on a pond,
Is one of my favorites that I've become quite fond.

The loons poetic call in a peaceful still lake,
Is a joyful sound that any day I will take.
The hoot of an owl as it pierces the night,
Is a soothing tone that makes you feel all right.

The robin, sparrow, lark & the golden finch,
Their songs fill the air & will do in a pinch.
So as the morning begins & the sun is sprawling,
I hope you enjoyed my tales of Nature's Calling.

My Favorite place

My Wife & I were talking one lazy day,
About the places we've been & often stayed.
We recalled our past travels & the things we've done,
As we ventured into places that were towards the sun.

We splashed in the ocean in an exotic location,
Took a cruise together into a new destination.
Sipped wine under the stars beside a gorgeous lake,
Planned our next adventure that we will soon make.

We saw the giant redwoods that stood so tall,
Stood by the river that flowed over Niagra Falls.
Lived in a quiet cabin in the Canadian woods,
The calming cries of the loon, all sounded so good.

Of all the places we've been, which do you like the best?
Just pick out a favorite, out of all the rest.
I thought for a moment & said that's an easy thing to do,
My all time favorite place, is right next to you.

My Destination

Up with the sun & gone with the wind,
Just to see what's around the bend.
Adventures abound for all of us,
So take a flight, bike, car or bus.

Take a road trip & drive for miles,
And stop to rest after a while.
Take a ride up high in the mountains,
Watch "Old Faithful" as she fountains.

Trek to Maine for some great seafood,
Or California to see the giant redwood.
Perhaps the "Grand Canyon" is just your thing,
Or relaxing in a pool in "Palm Springs".

Whether near or far just get away,
Plan more trips another day.
Whatever place you choose to reach,
My destination will be the beach.

My Amazing Life

In the Louvre I pondered at the Mona Lisa,
Climbed the spiral steps in the Tower of Pisa.
I gazed in wonder for almost an hour,
As I stood atop the Eiffel tower.

Inside the chapel Michelangelo painted there,
Got blessed by the Pope, in the Vatican Square.
Above the clouds in the Alps I learned to ski,
At the river Seine I drank French Chablis.

Drove along the coast of the Mediterranean sea,
A beautiful sight it was, for all of us to see.
The villages & people along the shores,
We took the time to shop several stores.

In Rome I walked the Appian Way,
The melted coins are still there today.
Our tour of the Coliseum was an amazing sight,
You could almost feel the gladiators fight.

I have witnessed some pretty amazing places,
And have met some beautiful faces.
I sat at home & explained to my Wife,
As I looked back on things & my amazing life.

Love Abounds

For the life of me I can't seem to understand,
What is going on throughout our land.
It seems there is no regard for human life,
Killing innocent people with guns & a knife.

We all need to take a close look as to why,
That people just seem to want to die.
When has society suddenly changed,
And decided to be so deranged.

We need to stop the finger pointing today,
And maybe listen to what people have to say.
Someone, somewhere holds the keys,
To stop all of these killing sprees.

Love & compassion has been replaced by hate,
But I believe that It's not to late.
We can turn this hatred all around,
And live in a world where love abounds.

Just Be Free

We sat on a mountain way up high,
Beneath a blanket of stars in the night sky.
A glass of merlot was just right,
My wife & I enjoyed this breathtaking sight.

The hustle & bustle of a city street,
The music & laughter just can't be beat.
We sipped our pinot in an outdoor café,
The city comes alive at night for play.

I love all these exciting new places,
Meeting new friends & old familiar faces.
Above all the places that we did reach,
My favorite one is always the beach.

There we sat with a drink in our hands,
Watching the waves as they lapped the sand.
This is the life that I want for me,
Laid back, easy & just be free.

Just A Few Things I love

I love the scent of a sweet summer rain,
The music as it taps on the window pane.
The lullaby of the tree frogs late at night,
Made an eerie sound in the pale moonlight.

I love the warmth of the mid day sun,
As it feeds my soul before it's done.
It is a time to be still & just breathe,
Take it all in before we have to leave.

I love the majestic beauty of the trees,
As they proudly stand adorned with their leaves.
I love the peace that summer can bring,
And the joyful song of the birds as they sing.

I love the fireflies at night as they glow,
As they dance and skitter to & fro.
The moon & the stars high up above,
These are just a few things that I love.

It's Winters Turn

Winter has reared its ugly head,
All the trees look barren & dead.
The North wind chills you to the bone,
The swirling cold air just makes you groan.

The windshield is covered in a layer of ice,
But using a scraper should suffice.
The new fallen snow has covered the road,
The plow trucks passed with salt in their load.

We have to bundle up from the bitter cold.
All the while knowing that this gets old.
We'll break out the shovels until it's through,
There's nothing more that we can do.

It looks like winter is here to stay,
The warmth of spring is so far away.
Our numbing hands feel like they burn,
That's what happens, when it is winters turn.

It Will All Go Away

The wind whispered through the trees,
As it made its way through with ease.
The summer breeze gently tousled my hair,
Then it moved on without worry nor care.

The summer heat was showing his might,
The clear blue sky with no clouds in sight.
The dog days of summer is approaching fast,
You could feel it on your skin from summer's blast.

The steady hum of air conditioners working to keep cool,
With sounds of children's laughter coming from a pool.
Everyone doing their best trying to beat the heat,
Those that succeed has accomplished quite a feat.

Some will stay indoors & complain to anyone,
While others will be outside & trying to have fun.
I relish in the Summers season each & every day,
Because I know too soon it will all go away.

It was always you

I never thought I'd find someone,
I thought love for me was all done.
All the heartache that I went through,
Somehow, led me straight to you.

You stood in the midst of my storm
Then I realized that our love took form.
As my world around me crumbled & fell,
It was you that saved me from that hell.

All you did was reach out your hand,
It was then I began to understand.
What true love was all about,
I knew my heart had no doubt.

When our eyes met on that amazing day,
All the pain had washed away.
I knew you were out there, that much was true,
But somehow I knew, it was always you.

Incredible Treasure

If you've never been to the ocean blue,
It's really something you must do.
It is indeed an incredible sight,
Either the sunset or dawn's early light.

It's vastness is something to behold,
The beauty it has, never grows old.
I remember the very first day that we met,
Was etched in my mind & I'll never forget.

I knew it was a place I would forever love,
As the seagulls & pelicans all flew above.
The roar of the surf crashing on the shore,
The feel of the sand from the ocean floor.

The salty taste caresses your lips,
The coolness of the water as you take a dip.
If you go there it will be nothing but pleasure.
I hope you can witness this incredible treasure.

In This House Dwells a Dog

There are nose marks on my sliding glass door,
And mud tracks on my Kitchen room floor.
Smudge marks on my cars windshield,
Dog hair on the seat, where he kneeled.

In my living room are toys to play,
Tug of war & fetch every day.
I pick up & the signs all day long,
Wondering where, I went wrong.

He wakes me up in the middle of the night,
So he can do his thing, in the moonlight.
He barks late at night & makes me mad,
Yet he melts my heart, when he looks so sad.

He makes me laugh, when he does his tricks,
Watching him run & fetch a stick.
He lies beside me as I rub his belly,
As we sit, & watch the telly.

As much as I gripe & complain,
Without him I wouldn't be the same.
All the little things that we share,
I know without him, I couldn't bear.

I love my dog & you can tell,
That this pet, has trained me well.
As I clean up crap in the morning fog,
Yes in this house dwells a dog.

In Our Dreams

We stood together with our feet in the sand,
And I quietly took hold of your hand.
We watched silently as the sun slipped into the sea,
As we stood breathless to witness the beauty.

The waves made their gentle lapping on the shore,
The gulls & pelicans flew no more.
An eerie calm had taken over the beach,
As the light slowly faded from it's reach.

The dusk was a mere glow as it said good night,
The stars & moon had emerged to their height.
Nothing in this world compares to this sight,
As the darkness ascended over the light.

I put my arm around you & kissed your head,
There will be other sunsets for us ahead.
We may never view this sight again it seems,
But we will forever replay it, in our dreams.

In my Arms

I've seen a lot of beauty with my eyes through the years,
Things that made my eyes well up with tears.
Our world is full of some pretty amazing sights,
From a blazing sunrise to star lit nights.

The oceans deep with their tumbling waves,
To the deep and dark mysterious caves.
The vast desert with the dunes of sand,
The man made objects that dot our land.

All of these things make you swell with pride,
That are on this earth that we all abide.
But not one of these things can compare,
To what I held in my arms with gentle care.

I held God's greatest gift in a hospital hall,
The miracle of birth that he gave us all.
My newborn baby that I held so tight,
In my arms laid the most perfect sight.

I'll be Alright

Oh Summer, I miss you so,
Under a blanket & looking out at the snow.
A steaming cup of coffee in my hands,
Slowly gazing at winters wonderland.

It is indeed pretty but I don't like the cold,
These months seem to drag & I am getting old.
Even the dog doesn't care for it,
She won't go outside even for a bit.

I relive the moments basking in the sun,
Everyone outside & having fun.
Tee shirt & shorts are the normal wear,
Barefoot or sandals & flip flops if you dare.

But alas, I'll suffer through this arctic blast,
Because winter as we know just won't last.
Sighing to myself I pull the blanket tight,
Summer will be here & I'll be alright.

I'll always Love You

You always know the right things to say,
When I am having, a very bad day.
You lift me up when I am down,
Even when you aren't around.

I love the way you love us all,
When the world around us begins to fall.
You are always there to see us through,
No matter what it is, we try to do.

When problems around us seem to arise,
You always seem to be so wise.
You manage somehow to keep us intact,
That my Dear, is a true fact.

I know sometimes things get rough,
And life often is very tough.
But you always seem to know what to do,
That is why I'll always love you.

I Sometimes Wish

I sat outside in the early morning light,
Coffee in hand, enjoying the sight.
An early breeze wafted through my hair,
Made a tousled look but I didn't care.

The bright blue sky high above me,
Was a welcome sight as any could be.
I watched a hawk glide high in the sky,
Until he decided to pass on by.

An occasional hum of a passing car,
As they made their travels near or far.
A beep or a wave as they pass,
Then move on with their foot on the gas.

I guess it's time for me to move on,
Until tomorrow morning just after dawn.
I know this day will soon be my past,
But sometimes I wished they would last.

I Remember When

I remember when I was just a young lad,
How I couldn't wait to go fishing, with my dad.
Those days are gone & now in my past,
But oh how those memories seem to last.

We would go to the creek & sit for hours,
Watching our bobbers & smelling the flowers.
I remember catching blue gills all day long,
Or an occasional bass that fought real strong.

I remember falling in the water & getting soaked,
Later on at home he made me the joke.
I kept him busy with snags & tangles,
As I watched him fish all the angles.

I learned a lot as I watched him fish,
To be as good as him, was my wish.
As I look back & take the time to reflect,
I admire his patience with due respect.

As I grew from a bobber and fished a lure,
I will always remember him, that's for sure.
When I watch my Son reel a fish in,
I smile to myself & remember when.

For my Father Carl,
From his Son Curt

I Love the Summer

The sky was the bluest I've ever seen.
The sun pierced the air creating a scene.
The trees were emerald & stood tall,
They would remain that way until the Fall.

The flower beds were ablaze with various hues,
Their blossoms adorned with the different blues.
The crimson roses nestled in a trellis,
The purple flox grew overzealous.

The lawns were decorated with the various things,
Creating the beauty that only Summer brings.
The vegetable gardens are flourishing,
Eating their bounty is quite nourishing.

The berries plants are bursting with their fruit,
They are delicious & looking so cute.
I love this season with all of it's wonder,
Of course this is the reasons I love the Summer.

I Love the Night

Once the sun goes down & we lose its light,
It is without a doubt, a beautiful sight.
The sky is adorned with the stars above,
The moonlight pierces the night with its love.

The winds of summer have ceased to blow,
Causing a stillness to the world below.
The sounds of Summer have grown silently still,
Creating a quietness so calm & tranquil.

The air is cooling from the sun's heat,
A refreshing change that can't be beat.
The fireflies create a scene & add the beauty,
As their lights flash, they go about their duty.

The serenity in the night I have found,
Is the one reason I love to be around.
In this amazing realm I feel just right,
That my friends is why, I love the night.

I just need to get away

I need to get away as soon as I can,
Somewhere exotic in a far away land.
Visit a beach with a clear blue sky,
Watch the seagulls as they fly by.

Lay on the beach & get a tan,
Sun glasses on & toes in the sand.
The gentle lapping of the waves on shore,
A dream any man could long for.

With a pina colada so cold on my lips,
Brings a smile to my face after a sip.
Sighing to myself how great life can be,
As I watched the sunset into the sea.

The phone woke me up out of my dream,
The boss is calling for me it seemed.
I dialed my travel agent & just had to say,
Oh man, I just need to get away.

How Beautiful

How beautiful the firefly on a mid-summers night,
It's greenish eerie glow indeed a beautiful sight.
I peered out my back door to the fields below,
Silently viewing the ever-constant glow.

As I sat perched contently viewing their dance,
They swirled and twirled lighting by chance.
Then the most amazing and incredible event,
As if to them a message was sent.

They seemed to gather and fill up my trees,
It was something I thought I'd never see.
Lights flashed like diamonds to and fro,
As in the sunlight of a new fallen snow.

I was transfixed in my doorway unable to leave,
Ash the lightshow continued its improbably weave.
There were thousands upon thousands so bountiful,
I stayed longer still and muttered "How Beautiful".

Food for Your Mind

I find that music really gives me what I need,
When my mind just needs to be freed.
Just put the headphones on & close your eyes,
You may be taken away & be surprised.

The soulful blues of a rhythmic beat,
Can often soothe & be quite a treat.
The vibe & sound of a steel guitar,
Can immerse your sensations by far.

The iconic voices that sing the blues,
Or the folkish duets that give us tunes.
The country twang if you wish to choose,
Music is a something you shouldn't lose.

No matter what kind you like to listen to,
This is something we all should do.
I guess it's something we all should find,
And that it really is food for your mind.

Enjoy the Wine

Crisp & light also refreshing,
Sipping wine has been a blessing.
The aromas on the nose it does sing,
Of the flavors that each bottle brings.

The vineyards that grow on our land,
Is in each glass we hold in our hand.
The flavors of the grapes on the vine,
Makes for a fine bottle of wine.

The swirl, scent & colorful hue,
All add to the taste, waiting for you.
When you raise your glass to the light,
Is indeed such a beautiful sight.

Salute, toast, & many cheers,
Is indeed music to your ears.
Because the harvest, will soon pass.
Enjoy the wine & fill your glass.

Engrave My Soul

At the foot of a mountain in a small trout stream,
I peered through the fog at a distant sunbeam.
The fog was lifting from the forest floor,
Creating a scene, like never before.

I watched in awe as the mountain awoke,
Picturesque as it was not a word I spoke.
The beauty of this memory was so serene,
Breathtakingly I stood absorbing the scene.

I stood in the stillness of dawn's early light,
Feeling the wonderment of this beautiful sight.
The peace that engulfed me was second to none,
Surrounded by the warmth of the morning sun.

In my memory I etched this fabulous day,
As a keepsake for me as I made my way.
As the fog gave way in a gentle roll,
This sight would forever engrave my soul.

Coffee Cup

I hope you will miss me when I'm gone,
But I don't want you to mourn for very long.
Go & live the rest of your life without me,
Travel, love, live & just be free.

I want you to smile & remember our time,
What our love was like while in its prime.
I want you to know that I loved it all,
And I wouldn't change a thing that I recall.

I hope that you never forget the love we had,
And NEVER about that, ever feel bad.
It is a beautiful thing & we were blessed.
To have each other when things were stressed.

I will be watching from up above,
So look up and smile at me my love.
When life get's hard & too much to bear,
Just look for my coffee cup by my chair.

At the Park

Sitting at the park watching the kids play,
It was a gorgeous summer day.
The kids were loudly running to & fro,
As kids always do you know.

The ball players were busy practicing their game,
The smiles made me happy that we came.
The swings were busy as they flew to the sky,
As if they knew it was their time to fly.

The blue sky & the emerald trees,
The park was indeed the place to be.
Running in circles they began to shout.
The slides & the monkey bars was quite a workout.

I sat on a bench so I could view this sight.
I bet they sleep very well tonight,
I imagine we'll be here close to dark,
But it was a wonderful day at the park.

At Night

Have you ever been on the beach at night?
It is indeed quite a beautiful sight.
The stars, sand, the moon & sea,
Is a magical place for all to be.

I could spend hours taking it all in,
Whether alone or with a friend.
The calming affect of waves on the shore,
Will forever bring you back for more.

Lovers will walk the beach hand in hand,
Stop occasionally for a kiss in the sand.
Some just like a lovely night stroll,
Walking with the tide as it rolls.

It's pure magic being in that place,
For peace of mind from the human race.
The beach makes everything alright,
When your soul coincides with the beach at night.

Asleep in our Bed

In my arms Your body had twitched as you fell asleep,
Your muscles relaxed as the trance went deep.
The scent of your hair as I held you tight,
where you would remain until dawn's early light.

Holding you close is life's greatest gift,
It makes my heart swell & lift.
The contentment I feel that surrounds our life,
Makes me happy we're Husband & Wife.

I kissed your forehead as you silently slept,
Etched in my memory & forever kept.
A smile quietly caressed my face,
With you in my arms there's no better place.

The night overcame me and I softly sighed,
Sleep took control as I closed my eyes.
Thoughts of you danced through my head,
Intertwined with you, asleep in our bed.